FINGERPRINTS

FINGERPRINTS

C. Obasare

Library of Congress Control Number: 2010911572
ISBN: Hardcover 978-1-4535-5316-9
Softcover 978-1-4535-5315-2
Ebook 978-1-4535-5317-6

This book was printed in the United States of America.

To order additional copies of this book, contact:
Xlibris Corporation
0-800-644-6988
www.xlibrispublishing.co.uk
Orders@xlibrispublishing.co.uk
300739

Foreword

Everyone has a unique set of fingerprints that usually leave behind an impression or mark on things. The mark that is left behind is sometimes used as evidence to tell a story for some unsolved mystery, which may ultimately lead to the discovery of the truth.

The poetry within *Fingerprints* is a unique collection that has left an impression on the minds and hearts of many. It attempts to find truth through the simple things. These words have left many asking questions, inspired some for the journey ahead and consoled others through difficult or perplexing times. Within *Fingerprints* is a vast spectrum of poems that span from, "Skintimate" moments, to the frustrating, "Where was God?" questionable times, without forgetting that we are all here, "For the Children".

Some poems will speak more to certain readers than others, but bear in mind that every stanza of each poem echoes the voice of the poet, in an attempt to still a spiralling world as too quickly it fades away. It attempts to find the words to echo the pain, joy, emptiness, longing, destitution or dense sadness that sometimes clouds us up inside. These are words to be enjoyed and shared or even contested and challenged. The poet's ultimate desire is that *Fingerprints,* which is now in your hands, leaves an impression on you and also compels you to make your own mark on things.

To My Family

The Grand Climax

Deep within
The constraints of the mind
Lies an innate desire
To explore and to find

What will be found
Only time can tell
Not all will find answers
From life's wishing well

As seasons change
And time draws nigh
Our longing, this world
Cannot satisfy

I know I can hardly
Wait for the time
For Him to cross over
And finally be mine

Atonement will come
Loneliness will cease
His aureole
Will fill me with peace

He won't be like Judas
Betray me with a kiss
My bridegroom will truly
Be sui generis.

His touch will be mild
His kiss so sweet
Like honey to my lips
Oil to my feet

His Spirit will grip
My body like a glove
And make me cry out
This must be true love!

My hunger will vanish
Nowhere to be found
New love in Him
Will quickly abound

My thirst will be quenched
My fire relit
My body transformed
Much more than a bit

The climax will come
My heart will sing!
Daylight, i'll see
You never again

Great earthquakes shall surface
With peals of thunder
And flashes of lightning
That will make me shudder!

Large bodies of water
Will be transformed
Into seas of blood
They all shall reform

Then all that I see
Will suddenly turn dim
My eyes will be closed
It will feel like a sin

There will appear
A new heaven and earth
Shining like jasper
Overflowing with worth

Its brilliance, more glorious
Than any dazzling light
Then no other will I see
But my Jesus Christ

I Do

Lord, what if you said
I will never marry
Or this bowl of a belly
Have no baby to carry

These hand-crafted palms
Will never caress
Or even be held
In blissful romance

What if blind Bartemeus
Never spat in that mud
Would he still be blind?
Would you still be God?

Of course this sounds strange
But mud is like marriage
Not our ultimate aim
But simply an agent

Lord, if I never become
Who I always wanted to be
Or never feel the warmth
Of another human being

My purpose remains unchanged
My calling in you fixed
You are my real surname
Despite what others may think

You are author and publisher
Of this book called life
You have all there is
And have been far too kind

Marriage has become an idol
But I'd rather the real thing
Like my friend Bartemeus
I just want to see my king

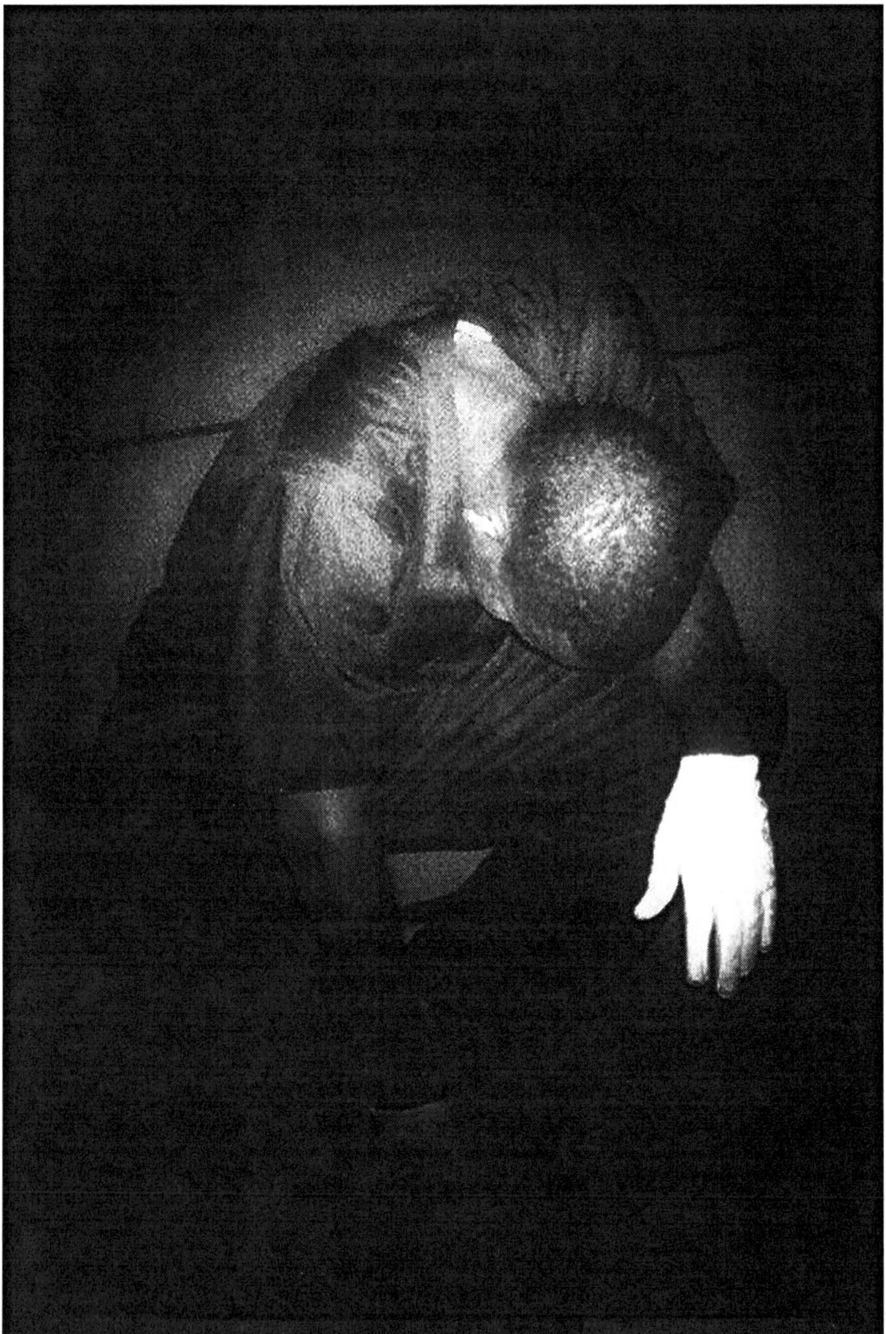

No Joke

I was half asleep
I was solving a riddle
The one with the cow
The cat and the fiddle

My body suddenly froze
I heard a loud peck
My pulse quickly rose
It thumped through my neck!

Then I heard no sound
But felt a slight pain
A prick in my back
That would leave a stain

A cascade of thoughts
Suddenly filled my mind
I should have said yes
I should have had time

Now what could be done
What would I become?
An infamous legend?
Or a legendary "bum"?

I had many chances
I cannot deny
But succumbed to advances
Of what caught my eye

It brought me such pleasure
Don't really know why
I had to keep bouncing
From stimuli to stimuli

One after the other
They came back to back
One wouldn't suffice
I always needed the pack

When would it stop?
When would it end?
The meaningless chase
The game of pretend!

I've become the epitome
Of fallen humanity
I created this tapestry
From velvety vanity

This is my story
I composed this symphony
It is no comedy
I wrote my destiny

God have no mercy

That Thing

Everybody has a thing
That completely captures the mind
That mystifies and intrigues
Defies every literary text

Its presence, strongly hypnotic
Euphoric and almost toxic
A sweet paralytic addiction
With escalating transitions

Another dimension of "high"
Which words have not surfaced to define
To some it is simply divine
And others, just so darn sweet

But one thing is for sure
It challenges your very core
Strips you blind and poor
Yet has you wanting more

Trapped in your own skin
Hostage to this "thing"
Chained to its rhythm
Enslaved by every ring

Whatever this thing may be
Whoever this shoe may fit
Ensure yourself of this
It's worthy of you to bits

The service of your lips
Your precious, valuable time
Your beautiful, young mind
Indeed, your entire life

Beyond the Veil

You gave me breath
You gave me life
And endless hope
Amidst trying times

Your every word
Was sacrosanct
Emitting a stillness
Like a hypnotic trance

I had no ideals
No lucid passion
But only this creed
Which you honed and fashioned

You were my Ali
My beer-belly champion
My Christopher Reeves
The sun's very radiance

But something went wrong
Somehow things changed
The light of your presence
Got caught in a haze

Now all that I see
Is only a figment
An elusive mould
With life-like pigment.

Your statutes like walls
Of incarceration
Your public appearance
Your primary distraction

If only I knew
Why seasons must change
Why rivers run dry
While some still remain

If time would retract
And your silence you erase
Dear Father if only
I could look upon your face

Paradox of Love

So many years gone by
Each one like a vapour
We live then we die
The in-between, most vital

Always give wholeheartedly
As if hearts come in spades
And with trust, do it carefully
The world is full of renegades

The most famous being friends
Who like intermittent streams
Cease to flow in dry season
And disappear at the sight of heat

Solitude has graciously
Clothed my weathered skin
But night pierces my bones
And torments my inner being

The ground thirsts my sweat
And cries for my tears
Like a lion on the prowl
Calamity senses my fears

I cry out! No answer
Just a busy signal
My meaningless existence
Like a cage of wrought metal

What am I that You
Consistently peruse my mind
Sanction my thoughts
Convict me all the time?

Why knit me with sinews
And build me with bones?
Only to break me
Then say you'll make me whole

I beg, take this life
And give to another
A more grateful friend
A more eloquent writer

For these lips lack terms
Of endearment to impart
These hands have no warmth
They lack a certain art

This heart has been wounded
And tattered with tears
It bleeds in sheer agony
And is tender with sores

So how can I stand
In a decibel of your thunder?
And how can I love You
Like a flipping, recurring decimal!

. . . yet I do.

Skintimate

I want to breathe you
And never let you go
I want to hold you
Until we form one mould

I want to trace you
Body, mind and soul
I want to lace you
Till we can't unfold

How lovely are
Your words to me
Like hot fudge
They melt me

When I'm with you
The world goes dim
You're all I see
Everything else spins

You stole my heart
Now I can't feel my feet
You paralyse me till
I forget to . . . breathe

How you invade me so
I trip over my tongue
When you say 'hello'

Whenever you're away
Something in me dies
The world turns to dust
Everything somehow sighs

If tomorrow never comes
And this is my last cry
I want you to know
You are my reason why

Somewhere . . .

Where children never cry
But laugh and giggle with joy
Where best friends never lie
Nor make your heart their toy

Where 'parents' is not a fraction
Nor a memory quickly forgotten
Where love is not a reaction
A feeling, nor bun in the oven

Where no one has to fear
That call we all dreadfully fear
Where no one has to hear
The words, "I'm so sorry dear"

Where time really heals
And in the end it's actually okay
Where joy never feels
Like a chance too risky to take

Where standing in the rain
Can remedy any hurt
Where love doesn't leave a stain
Or make you feel like dirt

Where this place exists
Only God would know
Where everyone finds solace
This place . . . I call it home

It's not you . . . it's me

It's not you I dislike
Nor your fingers through my hair
It's the feeling I get inside
More vital, its power I fear

It's like an innocent spark
A tiny speck of light
Tickling the air of the dark
Yet capable of great demise

Sometimes I truly wonder
"What if I just give in
Follow my natural desires
Not necessarily live in sin?"

God gave man ultimate dominion
So why not have it all?
No need to talk religion
Even Adam had to fall

Yet something doesn't feel right
Running after the insatiable high
Feeding the pleasures of sight
Till it leaves you flat-out dry

This life CAN make sense
This race can easily end
With God, now is the only tense
The past, a fogged-up dead-end

There is no switch or button
To drain past feelings of hurt
That pool like acid in the stomach
Since the heart has no room, just dirt

But His Spirit lives in my heart
And has made my temple his home
It feels like streams of diamonds
Flowing through my very bones

It silences my worries to a whisper
And sings to me each morning
It soothes like balls of cotton
When my eyes refuse to stop flooding

So how can I, even for a second
Submit or put on loan
A heart that's already betrothed
To the One who calls me His own

Sin-cerely

Need me
Love me
Whole me
Complete me

Look at me
Closely
Tell me
What are we

A parody
A symphony
Anomaly
An imagery

A chemistry
A tapestry
A comedy
A tragedy

Tell me
Truly
Look at me
Don't lie to me

Break me
Quickly
Severe me
Completely

Bury the
Monotony
Patiently
Drowning me

Let me be
History
Don't tell me
You miss me

I was made for you

Like water for chocolate
Like oil for my back
Like pins for a wicket
Like glue for a crack

I was created and fashioned
Sculpted and honed
Caressed with compassion
Hand-crafted from your bone

With a touch, I can relieve
The worries clouding your mind
With a look, I can ignite
The furnace behind those blinds

Every curve of this structure
Every groove of this mould
Is all but a fracture
Wanting to be whole

I am a fragile package
So be gentle with each part
Every inch of this lattice
Is God's signature work of art

Your duty is quite simple
Its execution quite pivotal
I know at times you'll stumble
But first get off of your pedestal

Look beyond your desires
Listen to my heart
I'll do all this love requires
I promise, till life departs

Simply Unfathomable

What if the sun got tired of shinning
The rain just felt like not falling
The wind decided to stop blowing
The earth got sick of spinning?

What if trees and tornadoes
Played "Pass roun' donkey"
And the loser had to take a hike
While lightning played "Go fishing"?

What if planets started playing tag?
What if mountains started dropping a few pounds?
What if oceans felt like greeting?
What if gravity got fed up of being down?

What if God grew weary of mercy
And quit playing our geometric mind games?
What if He no longer held His anger
And let it pour like sulphur rain?

What if God said, "No more forgiveness!
Get what you truly deserve
A taste of your own medicine
Enter a land of no return"?

What if God stopped being faithful
Gave dominion to nature instead?
What if He threw in the towel
And said we're as good as dead?

What if God refused to be caring
And ignored our cries of agony
Averted His eyes from the suffering
Looked down on the poor and needy?

What if God withheld His comfort
And scolded those who lost loved ones?
What if, utterly devoid of conscience
He passed us on the street like stray mongrels?

What if God gave up on love completely
And tossed it into hell's flames?
What if He retired in ultimate fury?
Who would step up to take the blame?

What if someone already did?

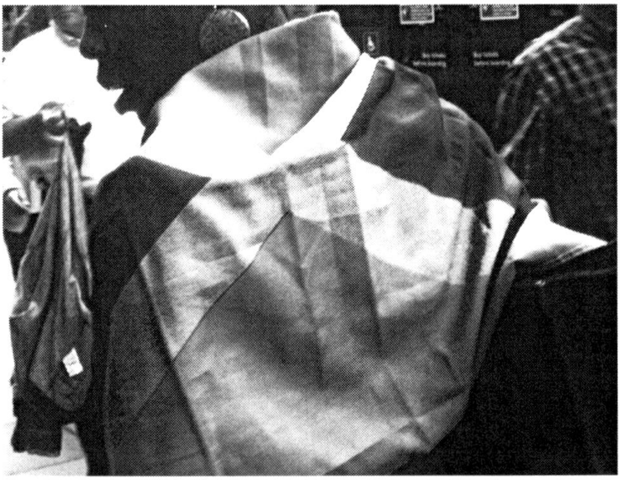

OUT OF MANY ONE PEOPLE

Jamaica: Land we love

Our land is rich with history
Of lives furnished with pain
Beyond the script of a movie
An evil no linguist can name
Our streets are asphalted with violence
Our kids have seen indescribable things
Our nights have not once heard silence
Our people have all felt death's sting

In this great "land we love"
We're plagued with something insane
Like a riddle left unsolved
Ferociously battling the brain
Has something sullied within
Buried beneath our bones
Stained with original sin
Why so quickly we race to our tombs?

An ailment or drug of some kind
Spreading like roots of a tree
Making our soil its hide
Boring holes a bullet-deep
Like a field of great force
It dominates our roads
Smashing without remorse
Evolutions and bugs the same

It ravages women of fullness
Who, savagely raped by pain
Feel their fibroid existence
Reluctantly fray away
It beats on hearts of men
Ripping apart with each stroke
The life of a brother or friend
With whom we not too long spoke

It weakens the heart of one loved
Ripe with severe cancer
Fading organ by organ
Or warped with convulsions of seizure?
Whether we are relatives of sorrow
Or scholars of feng shui
No one can ignore this horror
That slices our hearts like dull blades

"Amazing grace" doesn't quite cut it
When grief like a turbulent fall
Thumps till we're numb-struck
Still the currents refuse to withdraw
But God blessed us with today
And our mind's still in place
Blood still runs through these veins
So press till that timeless space

Another time, another place

There is rest
That sleep can't bring
There is relief
That tears cannot leak

There is peace
Beyond peace of mind
There is life
Not defined by our time

There is bondage
Without even a chain
There is freedom
That can still enslave

There is melody
No instrument can play
There is comfort
No words can convey

There is stillness
Not even air can paint
There is love
That never turns to hate

There is a world
That's not beneath our feet
Where there is no war
Promising us peace

Rest In Peace

Naked you came
Naked you depart
The Lord God gives
And He shall also part
Leaving behind this void
That aches like birth pains
And deepens with such loss
Too tender to even name

It yearns for your tears
And longs for your cries
But waits on your call
To let go them first
To release every groan
Mourn till it hurts
Weep till it burns
Leave no stone unturned

So let this time pass
For it must fully drain
Your every last thought
Of what could have been
How things might have changed
If only you said . . .
If only you did . . .
What wasn't in your head

That maybe somehow
There'd be another end
If only you saw
The 'hidden' trail of thread
But there were no clues
There were no crumbs
Nothing's left behind
Only up above

For no rationale
Could ever explain
How you're here today
And tomorrow just a name
Such knowledge is vast
Beyond your domain
But one thing's for sure
There's purpose in the pain

Whether you see it
Or not, it is there
Stark as the day
Dense as the air
So here's your charge
Starting today
Remember the lost
And not the pain

Cherish the times
Of laughter and cheer
And though we are gone
You're still in our prayers

A little more and a little less

Love a little more
Hate a little less
Try a little more
Give up a little less

Weep a little more
Grieve a little less
Express a little more
Withdraw a little less

Sing a little more
Yell a little less
Dance a little more
Run away a little less

Live a little more
Then we will die just a little less

For the Children

In every child
Is something divine
That money cannot buy
That ebay cannot price

Their innocence like petals
Their laughter like bubbles
Their mind like a vortex
With a world wind of questions

They should not pay
For what Daddy's done
They should not suffer
Because of Mummy's 'fun'

They entered this world
Through no course of their own
They had no say
They were never phoned

We are responsible
For this world they are in
So if at all possible
Change it for our kids

A Certain Nothing

Amidst the daily buzz
The smiles and the hugs
Floating in the air
Trapped in stifling despair

Our bubble of existence
With little incandescence
Spins through time and space
Like a dog-tail chase

In haste, we've lost our essence
Developed a cultured silence
Created a tangible presence
Of genuine emotional absence

Our smiles are painted lies
Our kindness, sweetened demise
Our eyes are like stained glass
Our laughter, rehearsed and masked

Coffee and white wine
The internet, DS, Playstation
Are drugs that make every attempt
To drown our human element

That part of us that's real
That part of us that feels
Both pain and joy so clean
We wonder if we're still here

For most, joy costs too much
And they would rather refrain
From even the slightest touch
That may just kindle a flame

Their hurt is buried so deep
In recesses beyond reach
Not even gravity can preach
To the depth of its own grief

They're wounded and can't see
Lying to themselves through their teeth
Hiding behind their own skin
With a certain nothing within

Missing

Love that forgives
Hearts that erase
Eyes without tears
Marriage without regrets

Father of ten
Mother of one
Sister with a pen
Brother without a gun

Children who haven't seen
What this world has done
Or what a human being
Can do in the name of fun

Government that is fair
Leaders that are true
People who don't fear
Speaking the painful truth

The world no longer sees
Its heart has turned to stone
Our Father is missing
And no one even knows

For the Unloved

Some people were born to lead
Some were born to follow
Some were purposed to sing
Some were born comedians

But were some born killers
Rapists, druggists and thieves
Were the mentally crippled
Destined even to be?

What about the others
The biblically sexual immoral
Or the old-aged ministers
Living with paedophilia

Is this the path they chose
Or is it entirely innate
Sin may live in our bones
But is it a permanent state?

Life is a slippery road
Everyone is prone to fall
But once it's not in our zone
We criticise and scorn

We are quick to condemn
And damn them all to hell
We label them by their sin
Yet televise them: comedy or suspense

Sadly, we have forgotten
A very crucial fact
The problem is not the person
It is solely the act

The person who is perhaps a victim
Of an inescapable past
A seemingly endless history
Of terror too cruel to ask

They are still truly human
They feel and hurt the same
They also have a mother
They even have a name

But do they deserve our love
Aren't they the ones to blame
Can't they just live unloved
Can they possibly change?

What if they weren't born this way
But this is what they have become
An unwanted piece of clay
Dying, just once, to feel love

Broken

I cannot forgive
I cannot forget
It hurts far too much
But I can do more

I cannot let go
I cannot erase
My past won't reload
But I can do more

I cannot not see
What's been done to me
Or uncry those tears
But I can do more

I cannot give up
What's been taken away
Tossed in the flames
But I can do more

I cannot breath
You took my breath away
Left me breathless
But I can do more

I cannot unfeel
The touch of desire
Or unspill its warmth
But I can do more

I cannot deny
I thirst for much more
Like water for chocolate
But I love You more

The Only One

If what I feel
Is remotely real
And not a dream
Then I must be ill

For nothing I have done
Is worthy of this
Rapturous delight
Unrelenting bliss

Beyond lethargy
Poetic ecstasy
Religious litany
Perpetual melancholy

Love so deep
No creed can claim
No bullet can reach
No language can frame

An illusion of sorts
That tickles the brain
A celestial rapport
Too elusive to name

A love that is pristine
Untouched, undefiled
Too often, it bleeds
Too often, it's kind

Love is God's kiss
A touch so riveting
It was made for spills
And the undeserving

I am indebted
Till I am dust
To a beauty unfading
A being unlike us

The one who never sleeps
The one who's Dad and Mom
The God of this great love
The One and Only One

The Two Doors

Life is full of moments
Each one's like a door
Behind which is a current
Threatening to change our course

A door as thick as pride
A door to endless rage
A door with a big "KEEP OUT" sign
A door to free from this cage

Whichever door it may be
We usually prefer it closed
Lest it dare reveal
A side we fear to know

A world outside our own
A truth that no one told
A land too far from home
A journey we must tread alone

Nothing about it intrigues
The body, mind or soul
But just like any old weed
It's hard to get it to go

Retreat is one step away
A door of a different kind
Reserved for anybody
Not ready to go under the knife

To die to self and shame
Which will only leave you blind
But then you'll always remain
A lifetime of doors behind

Words of Solomon

"Everything is meaningless
A chasing after the wind"
This was Solomon's solace
That life had no meaning

We toil beneath the sun
We battle with the wind
We taste of every plum
And quench totally nothing

People come and go
The earth still remains
The sun rises and folds
And hurries back again

The wind moves up and down
Round and round it blows
Its true path no one knows
Random as stocks seem to go

Streams flow into the sea
Yet it is never full
Our eyes have so much to see
Yet never have their fill

Wisdom brings sight to the mind
Ignorance leaves the world blind
But very few realise
Like the fool, the wise also die

They both will be forgotten
Their work or mess made equal
A past soon to be rewritten
By those with more or less wisdom

Wealth, fame and fortune
Are sweet but for a time
The celebrity life is a model
Of perfect psychological demise

"What does it profit a man,
To gain the world and lose his soul?"
To have beautiful, endless luxury
But not one place to call home?

Times are dark and hard
Life is growing seemingly cold
Its meaning is falling apart
Its centre can't seem to hold

Lost in the middle

In the middle of nowhere
Can be the sweetest place
Having no care in the world
And free to just be without

Lost in the beauty of nothing
The silence of time and space
Smiling when you should be crying
Singing when you should be dying

Forgetting all cares and worries
People who made you cry
People who never said sorry
But always 'apologise'

Leaving behind those burdens
That were never yours to bear
Those feelings of purest anger
That you should have never 'weared'

Let the future keep its distance
The past, its reminiscence
I am where I want to be
My present eternity

Where I am free to be without
A single care in the world
The sweetest place, no doubt
In the middle of nowhere

Where was God

Where were you
When slavery began
When thousands of lives
Turned to grains of sand

Where were you then
When Hitler was born
And the Nazi regime
Did indescribable horror

Columbine, West Virginia
Madrid, Oklahoma
London, Katrina
Haiti, Indonesia

The tragic nine-eleven
The beautiful princess Diana
Did You just watch from heaven
Did You even move a finger

AIDS, cancer, tumours
Why let them take our lives?
Where is this God of comfort
And love of which most testify

He replies, "Who darkens my counsel
With words you lack wisdom to chew
Without knowledge or even a fathom
Of what I have done and still do

"Where were you" He says, "when I laid
The foundation beneath your feet
What is that all around you
Show me the air that you breathe

"Tell me, if you understand
The components of light and time
Or the musical composition
In the heartbeat of every man

"Count the points on a line
Show me 'infinity' and 'undefined'
Touch gravity and tell it to unwind
Tell the sun not to glow in the night

"Mark off the dimensions of earth
The galaxy or the universe
Spin them around if you can
And point out which parts is yours

"Who has a claim that I must pay
To whom do I owe even a pound
My son paid it all on that day
Dare you question me, on what grounds!

It pains me every day
When boldly you ask
"Where am I?"
Now when I question your ways
With such boldness you shall reply!"

Lovely

I love you
Whether you call
Or not

I love you
No apologies
Full stop

I love you
Whether it's hot
Or cold

I love you
Full colour
Not sepia tone

I love you
With a warmth
In my heart

I love you
And ache
Each time we part

I love you
In a way
That makes me smile

I love you
Without fear of being hurt
This time

I love you
Like the sun sings
In the sky

I love you
Though people
Ask me why

I love you
Without any precise
Understanding of love

I love you
With a love
Only possible from above

Man without a face

I painted you once in my mind
With no ears, no lips, no eyes
Your heart, you said, was mine
My love, you said, was divine

Your hands were soft to touch
I felt secure in your clutch
You held me close so much
And there was never a rush

Each moment spent with you
Would always end too soon
Or feel like just too few
To share this love with you

Man without a face
I do not know your name
Or why each day it seems
For me, you slowly unveil

You have drawn me in
And hypnotised my will
You made me see some things
I thought were in the bin

Man without a face
I painted you in my mind
But never dreamt of this day
Where you actually come to life

Catch and Release

A memory
So fragile
Gentle
Warm

A touch
It tingles
Kindles
So soft

It floats
It bobs
On the wind
Up and down

It passes
With time
And soon
It is gone

I sat
I waited
Prayed
For your return

Now I stand
Unshaken
Fearing
The worst

Not that
You won't love me
Not that
You won't return

Not that
You will hurt me
Even worse
Than before

But something
More frightening
Bothers
My mind

That I must
Forget you
That I must
Go blind

Pretend
It never happened
Like a dream
Of some kind

As if
I never saw
Myself
Through your eyes

As if
We never walked
Through maze
And water, alike

As if
We never talked
And reasoned
Eye to eye

Yet this
Is what you want
So I
Won't make a fuss

This
Is my reward
For believing
In us

Lost and never found

Once I had a dream
That someday I could feel
Once I truly believed
That someone would see me

See even a beam
Hear when I scream
Undo this reel
Know how I truly feel

Is it a fantasy
Too far from reality
To see beyond tragedy
And hope for true beauty

Is it not insanity
To think in this humanity
That someone knows you thoroughly
When all you see is vanity

Once I really loved
And forever it will hurt
Because the one I loved
Has taken it to the dirt

What a friend

I am a contradiction
To my Christianity
Each day lacks vision
I am a living profanity

My words like sinking sand
My hope like withered grass
My purpose, I can't understand
My faith some sort of farce

"Whom have I in heaven but you?
Earth has nothing I desire besides you"
I wonder this world through and through
And still find out it's all about you

So why hide your face
Why scrutinise my ways
Who pressed erase
Oh ancient of days

Did I press the button
Did I say replace
Did I again do something
That made me an utter disgrace

That made my life go flat
That took you off the map
That makes me feel like crap
And placed me in this trap

Where my desires are screwed
I don't know who is who
My mind, my heart, my soul
To whom should I be true?

I asked you once before
And ask you once again
Why is life given
To a man whose way is hidden?

The paradoxical thing
Is I can't let you go
I cling to you like skin
Afraid to even grow

I just wish you were right here
So I know it will be okay
And through this living nightmare
Hold me till its day

I don't know what I've done
Or what I have become
Why you seem so cold
Why I'm on constant hold

I'm sorry my love was jaded
I let life get to my head
I want you back un-shaded
Like when you called me friend

Come back to me

Once I held you
I felt you
We touched too
Even moulded smooth

But my love couldn't hold you
Melt you
Or keep you
From going soon

Deep within I knew
Life would soon change tune
This symphony I well knew
Stronger than the blues

What once was in my hand
Is sifting now like sand
This bittersweet romance
Was only but a trance

A dance to time and space
A lovely, warm embrace
Beauty, I refuse to retrace
Whenever I see your face

Love it's said is something
If you give it away
It comes right back to you
Then it's there to stay

So I have done my part
And I can only pray
That now you have my heart
You won't let me turn away

The Mother Half

Foxes have holes
Birds have nests
Pigs have pens
Dogs have kennels

Humans have houses
Very few call homes
Arguments and quarrels
The only 'peace' they know

Children go to school
Learn add and multiply
But how can they understand
Amidst subtract and divide

To most, parents is a fraction
An inconceivable whole
A selfish, narrow-minded division
Even Einstein couldn't code

Some children are left 'to be continued'
Discarded like unwanted hair
Their parents did conception
And left the rest to their care

Very few are lucky
Some are even blessed
To have somewhere truly
Where they can find rest

"Many women do noble things
But you surpass them all"
I'm honoured to know such a being
Whose love always catches my fall

Foxes have holes
Birds have nests
But I have a mother
And pray for the rest

All about you

I like to make you happy
I like to make you smile
I like to make you see me
I'd like to be your bride

You have all that you want
Everything you dreamed of
Satisfaction in your heart
And me, trophy in arm

Love, they say, is patient
Love, they say, is kind
True love, I think, is ancient
It ages like fine wine

The truest kind is selfless
Not a game of give and take
But humans, we are selfish
We want to win each take

Whenever I love
I put you above
So much so I drop
Myself off the map

I service your wants
I polish your fame
I edit the spots
I take all the blame

I wish I were happy
I wish I could smile
I wish you were something
I also wished last time

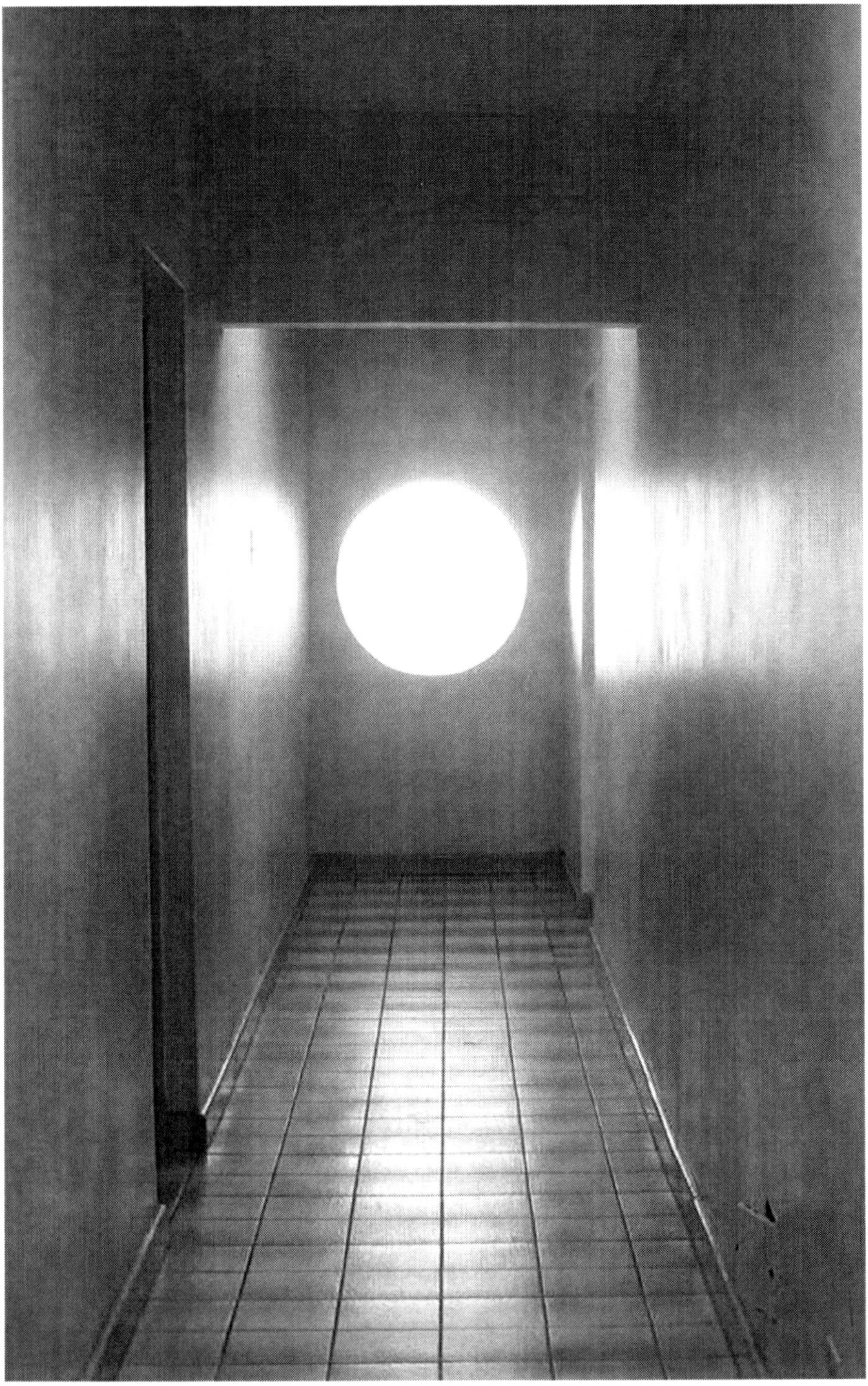

Gone

I want to say your name
This time without falling apart
I want to see your face
Outside that expensive cast

I want to hold your hand
And not let it slip away
I want to say those words
I always said I should say

I want to say hello
That time you were online
I want to give you a minute
Not be in a rush this time

I want to shut my mouth
And actually let you speak
I want to hear the silence
Of rivers they say run deep

I know there is a symphony
A beautiful unweaving
As people come and go
In and out like breathing

From the pit of the stomach
Is a song we all know
Unpalatable sorrow
An intensely climatic woe

Each day that dies
Leaves many soldiers behind
But as we live out life
Let's keep their memory alive

My Precious

I pray that you will find
All that is good in life
Blessings you perhaps thought
Would not be yours this time

May love seek you and find you
Erase the hurt that tore you
Bless the dirt that bore you
And unearth the wisdom inside you

I pray when you smile
It will come from within
Instead of self-denial
Claiming all is well

I pray this chapter of life
Will not stay this way forever
I pray you see its purpose
And because of it grow stronger

I pray you will see yourself
As beautiful as you are
Instead of that warped vision
Of tapestrated scars

I pray you listen to that voice
That says you're wonderfully made
A diamond in the rough
A refreshing glass of lemonade

I pray you learn to love life
And live it to the fullest
Never give half-way
And always choose to be honest

I pray you never treat people
The way you have been treated
Though it may be tempting
How else will they see Jesus?

I pray you learn to love yourself
Just the way you are
Never fear speaking your mind
Or voicing what is on your heart

I pray you grow to be
All you ever wanted to be
And see all the wonderful things
In the world there is to see

I pray this world may know
The beautiful soul you are
More precious than chests of gold
More radiant than the stars

I pray you will be a blessing
Now you read this through
Knowing someone took a minute
To write it just for you

Beautiful One

Every tear you cry
Tears my world apart
It saturates my sky
And pierces my heart

I hurt when you hurt
I cry when you cry
I watch you toss dirt
And ask yourself why

Sometimes I wish you knew
How much I really love you
And how it pleases me
To watch you love as you do

When you were a child
I saw your inner conviction
You fought with your whole heart
And moved with holy compassion

You learned at such a young age
The true meaning of being one
Without effort you became
Your solitary companion

Not once did I leave you
Though no one understood you
I hid in every corner with you
Because, my child, I loved you

I am the one who made you
I moulded your very birth
I kissed your soul with life
And breathed in you great worth

I placed heaven in your eyes
Summer in your smile
Mother in your touch
Beauty so divine

It brings me tears when I think
How much I really love you
I wish you truly knew
What I see as I look at you

Undo me

What shall I say
That I have not said
What can I utter
That won't be misled

What can I ask for
That has not been given
How can I answer
Me, my big question

My biggest intention
My only objection
My greatest distraction
Your beautiful creation

My life sentence is a full stop
Surrounded by do not's
Filled with can not's
Sprinkled with will not's

Not "To have and to hold"
Or "Bone of my bone"
"I won't leave you alone"
"Your heart is my home"

Either way, it's a lie
Everyone can deceive
With words like chamomile
And hearts like killer weeds

So how can I pray
When I don't believe
It's not like a braid
That I can just weave

It's not like a battery
That I can recharge
Or a computer
That I can restart

Where is the source
That will quench my thirst
And undo this curse
That's left me in reverse

Sweet nothing

Can I think of you and pray that you are enjoying life without me
Can I hold a child in my arms and not wish it were ours

Can I brandish a smile without wondering what you are doing at that precise moment,
and hope you felt its radiance wherever you are and are smiling back

Can I snuggle in at nights and refuse to entertain the tender thought of your warmth cradling me to sleep

Can I wake up in the morning and still say a prayer for you with a smile on my face

Can I reminisce the past and thank God it happened and believe better will come

Can I truly believe that there is someone who really loves me, will never hurt me, wants to grow old with me and will never regret me . . . like you once said?

Awesome Wonder

It is no secret
The sky is blue
The grass is green
The earth in between

The sea sits flat
Obeys the sound
The inaudible speech
That follows us around

The heavens declare it
The skies proclaim it
The sun radiates it
The world deflects it

I can't mistake it
I can't replace it
Though I fight it
I can't escape it

As silent as it is
It pierces my mind
Drills my ignorance
Numbs me blind

I sit and watch
The earth go round
The sky sit still
A free motion picture

Yours Truly

You want to find
A home that never fades
A hug that never goes
A hand that never waves

A pillow that holds you close
Rests your troubled mind
Softens through to your toes
Cushions your dreams inside

You want to believe, truly believe
That you are capable, more than able
To do exceedingly, more abundantly
Above and beyond your mental galaxy

You want to have
You want to hold
The life you never met
The past you rewrote

You are still waiting
Wanting and hoping
Dreaming and praying
Dying believing

You want it to end
The trying, the struggling
The failing, the breaking
Driving you crazy

You crave delight
Splendour in the light
You want perfection
Not governed by sight

You still pour out
Body, mind and soul
Like paint on a canvas
Hoping to God it will look whole

Pieces Of Me

A hearty embrace . . . a hand of comfort . . . a warm cup of cider . . . the sun streaming through the window . . . the sound of waves as they whisper sweet nothings to my toes . . . the sweet smell of rain on hot soil . . . the sound of birds singing in the morning . . . the hush of silent rivers that run deep . . . the bittersweet crash of cold water against my skin . . . the taste of mango freshly plucked from the tree . . . the burst of flavour from a mouth-watering slice of watermelon . . . the touch of heaven in each petal of a cherry blossom . . .

LaVergne, TN USA
21 October 2010
201806LV00001B/83/P

9 781453 553152